To Find a Killer

The Homophobic Murders of

Norma and Maria Hurtado

and the LGBT Rights Movement

Douglas Greco

To Find a Killer

The Homophobic Murders of
Norma and Maria Hurtado
and the LGBT Rights Movement

GAUDIUM

Gaudium Publishing

Las Vegas ◊ Chicago ◊ Palm Beach

Published in the United States of America by
Histria Books
7181 N. Hualapai Way, Ste. 130-86
Las Vegas, NV 89166 U.S.A
HistriaBooks.com

Gaudium Publishing is an imprint of Histria Books.
Titles published under the imprints of Histria Books are
distributed worldwide.

Library of Congress Control Number: 2023932045

ISBN 978-1-59211-298-2 (softbound)
ISBN 978-1-59211-359-0 (eBook)

Contents

Introduction

From the moment I picked up the newspaper and recognized that my former student was the victim of an anti-LGBT murder, I struggled to connect all the dots. I had organized for a decade with one of the most effective grassroots networks for economic justice, and at the same time, as a gay man, had been an active supporter of LGBT organizations and student of the LGBT rights movement. Though these murders occurred in a low-income, immigrant neighborhood I had been organizing in, it wasn't clear how the intersection of homophobia, economic segregation, race, and immigration status all were at play. Calls by local and national LGBT groups labeling this a hate crime, while necessary and true, were insufficient in my mind to identify and address all the underlying factors at work. My faith in writing this book has been that leaning into the particulars of the Hurtado murders could provide me with answers to these broader, more systemic questions I grappled with.

I draw the first chapter from my already published narrative account of the Hurtado murders in 2011, based on my first-hand knowledge of the case, interviews, and media accounts of the murder and trial. 2011 saw a record twenty-seven anti-LGBT murders, and 2010 was marked by the high-profile "September Suicides," a spate of high-profile LGBT youth deaths by suicide. I argue that this particularly tragic period woke the nation up to the horrific toll of continued anti-LGBT bias and created the space for the monumental shift in public opinion and historic victories in LGBT civil rights over the next five years. By pointing to the continued violence against the LGBT community, with murders of transgender individuals today rivaling the number of overall anti-LGBT murders in 2011, I argue that recent civil rights victories are insufficient to reduce the continued violence against members of our community like Norma Hurtado.

Rather than simply blaming homophobia for the Hurtado murders, in the second chapter I explore models of intersectionality that dig deeper into potential underlying factors. Sociologist Doug Massey's framework of categorical inequality, and how disparities along the lines of race, class, sex, and family structure multiply when they co-exist in neighborhoods like Dove Springs, provides a useful framework for understanding the compounded stratification many in the LGBT community face. Norma was from a low-income neighborhood, female, an immigrant, and gay. Drawing also from the hate crimes research of Rafaela Dancygier and others, I argue that although Norma was "out" and living in a progressive city like Austin, she was perceived as a threat to the perpetrator, who attended a conservative evangelical immigrant church and lived in a neighborhood that was socio-economically marginalized from the rest of the city.

Since Massey's framework doesn't explicitly address the LGBT community, though, where do we look for examples of this more intersectional approach specifically focused on LGBT rights? The international LGBT rights movement, with its emphasis not just on legal rights, but economic, health, social, and cultural rights, provides the most useful example. Grown out of the international human rights movement with its broad focus on the full sweep of human rights, rather than the legal rights-based U.S. LGBT movement, the international LGBT rights struggle was initiated by organizations like Human Rights Watch, Amnesty International, and international HIV/AIDS organizations starting in the 1990s. Though the U.S. movement has achieved monumental civil rights victories in the past decade on marriage equality, workplace non-discrimination, and anti-hate crimes legislation, in the third chapter I argue that the broader scope of rights of the international LGBT movement is the best lens through which to see the challenges for the LGBT community in the next phase of the movement.

Which of these rights should be the most central to the LGBT community's fight for equality and inclusion? Which is the most important? Lifting up what Hannah Arendt calls "the right to have rights", in the fourth chapter I argue that the fight to maintain our seat at the table in the American polity, the political community, is our most important work. This requires building the type of enduring political institutions that form leaders, teach democratic engagement, and build power to enable the LGBT community to continue to fight for all other rights. Drawing from my fifteen years-experience of broad-based institutional organizing with the Industrial Areas Foundation, I argue that civic and religious institutions have a central role in developing the type of organizations and leadership necessary for this struggle.

Historian Margot Canaday identifies the middle of the twentieth century as one of the most repressive periods in American LGBT history, yet this period also gives us some of our most heroic LGBT leaders, whose work exemplifies key fundamentals in political organizing. The fifth chapter explores key political organizing strategies employed by several of these figures. José Sarria, a celebrated drag performer and activist in 1950s-60s San Francisco, cunningly organized gay bars and created new political organizations to push back on police repression. Craig Rodwell, an early activist in the New York City Homophile Movement, developed his leadership through direct action during the 1960s and leveraged the skills and relationships he built to bring national attention to the Stonewall Riots. Harvey Milk, the first openly LGBT person to hold elected office in the US understood the importance of broad-based coalitions to build the power necessary to counteract the business and government interests that marginalized the LGBT community and other disenfranchised groups. And key LGBT leaders like Bayard Rustin and Urvashi Vaid deployed these same principles in the fight for racial and economic justice more broadly. This look back in history can help prepare us for the fight ahead.

In the final chapter, I argue that the historic shifts in acceptance and inclusion of the LGBT community in the past decade, culminating in the Supreme Court's Obergefell ruling legalizing same-sex marriage, were our nation's response to the tragic spate of LGBT deaths by suicide in 2010 and a record number of anti-LGBT murders of 2011, including the Hurtado murders. Though many LGBT organizations have embraced an intersectional lens, especially after marriage equality was realized, like the California-based statewide equality organization I worked at in 2015-16, fewer have adopted the grassroots leadership development and broad-based institutional organizing fundamentals necessary to undo systemic and structural inequities across race, class, gender, and geography. Hate crimes like the Hurtado murders continue today in record numbers, underscoring this reality. This book attempts to not only understand the full scope of factors contributing to such tragedies but to also propose concrete and bold strategies to prevent them from happening again.

Chapter 1

Tragedy and Hope in Dove Springs: The Murders of Norma and Maria Hurtado

A look back at the 2011 Hurtado murders, a hate crime against the LGBT community, that examines how issues of race, religion, economic status, and homophobia are often intertwined.[1]

On April 18th, 2011, José Aviles approached the house of Maria and Norma Hurtado with an automatic pistol in his hand.[2] Maria and her 24-year-old daughter Norma lived in the working-class, immigrant neighborhood of Dove Springs in Austin, Texas. When Norma came to the door that

---

[1] First published in *Across the Margin* magazine May 8, 2020.

[2] *Austin American-Statesman*, "Dad Shot Two Women Over Daughter's Relationship", April 20, 2022, by Claudia Grisales.

night, Jose Aviles emptied fifteen rounds into her and another round into her mother, who had stepped in front of Norma to protect her. Both women died instantly.

At the time of her death, Norma had been in a romantic relationship with Aviles' daughter, Lidia, for over a year, and was open about her same-sex relationship. A manager at a Dove Springs Wendy's, Norma helped support her own parents as well as Lidia's daughter. José Aviles had been sending text messages to Norma over the preceding months, threatening to kill her. He wanted the relationship to end.

I taught Norma at Johnston High School in East Austin ten years prior to her murder. I recognized her face and remembered her name when I picked up the newspaper the day after the killings. My mind shot back to my ninth-grade classroom, Norma standing in front of my desk with her athletic build, confident smile, and deep brown eyes.

Her murder was among the record-high thirty anti-LGBT murders in 2011 in the United States, the highest number since such records were kept.[3] The majority of the victims were persons of color and transgender individuals, and like the Hurtado murders, many made local and national headlines. One example was Camila Guzman, a Latina transgender woman who was found stabbed to death and face down in her East Harlem, New York apartment.[4]

The previous fall the nation had seen a rash of at least ten high-profile deaths by suicide amongst teen and young adult members of the LGBT community, mostly due to anti-gay bullying.[5] "The September Suicides," as they would come to be known in the fall of 2010, included Seth Walsh, who was relentlessly bullied for being gay in school in a small town near Bakersfield in

---

[3] Huffington Post, "Highest Number Of Anti-Gay Murders Ever Reported In 2011: The National Coalition of Anti-Violence Programs." June 2nd, 2012, by Lila Shapiro.

[4] Queerty, "Transwoman Camila Guzman Literally Stabbed In The Back By Her Murdering Boyfriend". August 24th, 2011, by Daniel Villarreal.

[5] GLAAD Webpost, "The Tragedy of LGBT Teen Suicide," October 1st, 2010, by Angela Dallara.

California's Central Valley. Seth hanged himself on September 19th, spent the next ten days on life support, and died on September 28th.

The next several years saw a monumental shift in public opinion and acceptance of the LGBT community and a surge in support for LGBT rights, in large part due to increased advocacy and awareness on the part of the LGBT community and allies within the broader society. I believe this was largely our country's reaction to this horde of high-profile suicides by LGBT youth and young adults and anti-gay hate crimes in 2010-2011.

Despite the progress, the Hurtado murders remind us of the incredible cost of just two lives during this tragic time, and how issues of race, religion, economic status, and homophobia are not easily separated. The brutal murders also remind us of the ways in which families and communities respond to horrors in their community can help shape and catalyze a larger movement for equality and dignity.

Life in Dove Springs

Dove Springs was originally a white working-class neighborhood with 1950s-60s era gray brick, small ranch-style houses. Today it is mostly older housing developments and apartments, with more recent prefab houses built around its edges. Because of its cheap and abundant rental housing, it is home to lower-income residents, the majority immigrants from Mexico like the Hurtado and Aviles families. Dove Springs has no town center, just a few roads with strips of fast-food restaurants, dollar stores, check-cashing establishments, and small churches.

As a high school student, Norma was self-assured, athletic, and dressed sporty. She always looked you in the eye when you spoke with her. Though homophobic remarks could be fairly common at Johnston High, where I taught Norma in my ninth-grade geography class, Norma never seemed to hide her sexuality.

Norma started working at Wendy's when she was nineteen and continued for the next five years, eventually becoming a manager. She was popular with coworkers and her supervisors and had a wide circle of friends.

As a young adult, Norma also played competitive soccer, which seemingly formed the core of her social network. Pictures online show Norma with her friends and family together at parties, with her mom often crying happily. Norma consistently looked like the leader of the pack.[6]

It was at Wendy's that Norma met Lidia Aviles. Norma was twenty-three and Lidia was seventeen and raising her daughter, whom she had given birth to a few years earlier. They began seeing each other romantically, and when Lidia was eighteen, she and her daughter moved in with Norma and her parents, posting on Facebook that she and Norma could now be together in peace.

---

[6] YouTube video, "Maria y Norma Hurtado," 2011 by Isabel Alvarez.

Mounting Pressure

The situation with Lidia's family was far different than with Norma's. Her father, José Aviles, didn't approve of her relationship with Norma from the start, and increasingly pressured Lidia to break up with her. He would say it was because she was neglecting her motherly duties and her schoolwork when sneaking away to spend time with Norma. Lidia later said at her father's trial that he had a special relationship with his granddaughter, almost acting as if he was the child's father.

Lidia and her daughter moved in with Norma once she had turned eighteen, relieved that she was finally able to live with her girlfriend. José Aviles began to threaten Norma's life through text messages. He warned her to stay away from Lidia and felt that Lidia should focus on school and raising her daughter. Lidia felt the safest place for her and her daughter was at the Hurtado house.

Lidia's father attended an evangelical church in the neighborhood. Lidia had an older brother, and on least one occasion he came to the Hurtado house searching for his sister. Police had to intervene at the Hurtado house at least twice during the next several months. There was a report of a sexual assault in September and then a family disturbance in October, but they chalked it up to a family conflict.

Despite all this, the threatening text messages from Lidia's father continued.

7171 Dixie Drive

Most of the houses on Dixie Drive in Dove Springs are now gone, torn down after the horrific "Halloween Flood" which devastated the neighborhood in 2013. Aside from a few houses, the street now looks desolate. But to visualize the street on April 18th, 2011, you would have to imagine both sides filled with ranch-style, worn-down houses, and tree-barren yards.

At about 7 p.m. that evening, José Aviles and another man drove up to 7171 Dixie Drive in a dark green SUV. Aviles later claimed that they had come to get his daughter. Reports are unclear about the other man's role, though I spoke to the wife of a next-door neighbor who heard a car door slam just as the car pulled up, leading him to believe that José Aviles must have been the passenger, not the driver. Aviles then came to the door with an automatic pistol, knocked, and Norma's mother Maria opened the door. Aviles asked for his daughter, Lidia.

Maria yelled to the back of the house, where Lidia and Norma were in a room together, to let Lidia know her father was there. Instead of Lidia, Norma came to the front door and stood by her mother.[7] When Aviles saw Norma, he riddled her with fifteen bullets from his automatic pistol. Norma fell to the floor bleeding. At some point, Maria stepped in front of Norma to shield her. Aviles shot Maria in the neck, severing an artery, and she fell to the floor and died instantly. In a police interview, Aviles later said he would have continued shooting Norma if he had more ammunition.

---

[7] *Austin Chronicle*, "The Road Against Hate: The Hurtado Murders Measure The Distance Austin And Texas Must Travel." May 6th, 2011, by Jordan Smith.

Lidia ran to the door, and when she saw what had happened, she fell upon Norma, trying in vain to stop her bleeding. She then called 911, screaming. Aviles fled the scene. Neighbors had heard the shots and the screaming and came to the scene. Soon the police flooded the neighborhood and launched a manhunt.

Aviles, in his green SUV, eventually made his way to a relative's house. His relative later told police "José was nervous, intoxicated, and had a gun in his waistband."[8] Aviles repeated that he had "done" something and needed their help. His relative called the police.

The police interviewed Lidia who explained how her father disapproved of her relationship with Norma, and that there had been conflicts between them. A friend of Norma's told police about the threatening text messages Aviles sent Norma. "She stated that (the girlfriend's) parents have sent text messages threatening Norma because of the relationship."

---

[8] Grisales, "Dad Shot Two Women," April 20, 2011.

Aviles' wife, Roselia Martinez, and her son showed up at the scene of the crime that night. They told police that they were also looking for Aviles. Martinez said she believed he was drunk and that he owned an automatic pistol. Police searched for Aviles all night, in conjunction with the Lone Star Fugitive Task Force, the local arm of the U.S. Marshals Service.[9] Early Tuesday morning, about twelve hours after the murder, they located a Nissan Altima, associated with Aviles, in a carport in the town of St. Hedwig, in Eastern Bexar County, ninety minutes South of Austin and thirty minutes east of San Antonio.

According to the *San Antonio Express-News* "About 30 San Antonio police officers and U.S. Marshals, backed by canines and SAPD's helicopter Blue Eagle, surrounded Aviles at about 3:30 a.m., officials said, and he surrendered."

A friend and neighbor of the Hurtado family told me that almost all the neighbors, mostly

---

[9] *San Antonio Express News*, mysanantonio.com, "Austin Double-Murder Suspect Arrested in St. Hedwig." April 19, 2011.

monolingual Spanish speakers, declined to speak to the media. Curiously, however, later that day Aviles' wife, Roselia, let a reporter and photographer into her home for an interview. But a group of family members asked them to leave before Martinez could answer questions.

Aftermath

Two white caskets sat at the altar of Cristo Rey Catholic Church on Austin's East Side on April 25th, 2011. According to reporter Claudia Grisales of the *Austin-American Statesman*, over one hundred and fifty friends and family attended the Hurtado funeral, many wearing T-shirts that read, "Like a rainbow gone too soon, but never forgotten." Father Jayme Mathias, who eventually became a school board member in Austin, was the pastor. His sermon was affirming and one of inclusion. "Some take Bible verses out of their context, to reject some based on their sexual orientation."

The Hurtado murders first hit the local papers as a family squabble gone awry. As details emerged, the story changed. Norma's relationship with Aviles' daughter came center stage and it became clear — this was a hate crime.[10] Reaction from the community was swift.

Local LGBT groups were the first to speak out, joined by political and community leaders.[11] Members of the city's hate crime task force, created earlier that fall in response to an attack on two gay softball players in a city hall parking garage, weighed in. Eventually, it popped up in LGBT papers around the world. Even the president of Pisces Foods LP, the company that ran the Wendy's where Norma and Lidia worked, spoke on behalf of his employees, "They are in some disbelief, especially someone so important and well-liked in our group."

There was a candlelight vigil with about two hundred people outside of the Hurtado home on

---

[10] Smith, "Road Against Hate," May 6th, 2011.

[11] *Austin American-Statesman*, "Gay Rights Groups Want Shootings Prosecuted As Hate Crime," April 22, 2011, by Claudia Grisales.

Dixie Drive. Friends described Norma's mother Maria as her biggest champion.

During the time of the murders, I was the Lead Organizer of Austin Interfaith, a grassroots coalition of religious congregations, schools, and unions that had been working in Dove Springs on health and community safety issues. There had been a spate of murders in the neighborhood that year, so when I picked up the article on the Hurtado murders, I assumed it was part of the crime spree. And then I saw the pictures. I said to my boyfriend at the time, "I know who this is."

Chapter 2

The Role of Race, Class, and Sexuality in the Murders of Norma and Maria Hurtado

When I read the newspaper that April morning in 2011, I recognized Norma as a former high school student I had taught a decade earlier at Johnston High School in inner-city Austin. Immediately after the murder, a host of LGBT advocacy groups held a press conference and rightly denounced the murder as a hate crime. In the media, José Aviles was portrayed as a homophobic father intent on ending his daughter's lesbian relationship by killing her lover. Although the case was not prosecuted under the Texas hate crimes law since it would not have increased the perpetrator's sentence, in December of 2012 Aviles was convicted of capital murder and sentenced to life in prison without parole.

Largely unexplored in initial media reports
and subsequent analyses of the murders were the
issues of race and class. Norma and Maria
Hurtado were working-class Hispanic women
and Aviles and his daughter were undocumented
immigrants.[12] Both families lived less than a mile
from each other in the Dove Springs neighborhood of Southeast Austin, which has one of the
highest poverty rates and crime rates in the city.[13]
Norma, who was open about her sexuality to her
family, attended a high school notorious for its
instability and poor academic performance.[14] José
Aviles had attended an evangelical church in

---

[12] It is unclear from media reports what Norma and Maria
Hurtado's citizenship status was.

[13] Castillo, Juan, "Dove Springs Facing Crossroads", *Austin-
American Statesman* newspaper article. December 6th, 2009.

[14] Johnston High School was ordered to be closed by Texas
Education Commissioner Robert Scott in 2008, with a new
school, Eastside Memorial High, opening soon after at the
same facility.

Dove Springs.[15] While the issues of gay rights and homophobia are central to this case, so are the issues of race and class. In fact, they are inextricably linked. Through this case, I will explore the limits of addressing issues affecting LGBT persons from a traditional gay rights perspective. I propose that situating equal rights for LGBT persons within a larger context of race, class, and family structure provides a much fuller framework for understanding this case specifically, as well as issues affecting LGBT persons more generally.

The "Rights" Approach

Individual and Minority Group Rights

Debates on multicultural policy over the past several years have focused on the tension between minority group rights and the rights of individuals within those groups. Susan Moller Okin

---

[15] This was according to initial media reports. Though the Hurtados' funeral was at a Catholic church, Aviles evidently attended a non-denominational evangelical congregation.

argues that individual rights within a minority group, specifically women's rights, should trump the rights of a minority group when membership in that group limits the basic freedom of individuals.[16] Similarly, Christian Joppke argues that liberal pluralistic nation-states should use equality and liberty, not special group rights, as a binding principle.[17] Will Kymlicka argues, however, that liberal egalitarians can also accept a set of special group rights which make a claim on the larger society in order to reduce vulnerability and redress historical injustices.[18] This tension between individual and group rights helps explain some of the dynamics operating in the Hurtado murders.

---

[16] Okin, Susan. *Is Multiculturalism Bad for Women*, Princeton University Press: Princeton New Jersey, 1999.

[17] Joppke, Christian. "The Retreat of Multiculturalism in the Liberal State: Theory and Policy", p 254. *The British Journal of Sociology*, 2004. Volume 55 Issue 2.

[18] Kymlicka, Will. "Liberal Complacencies", within *Is Multiculturalism Bad for Women?* p. 31. Princeton University Press: Princeton New Jersey.

Both the Hurtado and Aviles families lived in a mostly Mexican American immigrant neighborhood. Predominantly Catholic and evangelical Christian, this community likely had a more traditional conception of family and marriage than the broader community of Austin. Austin is generally seen as one of the most culturally and politically liberal cities in Texas. Given that José Aviles was a monolingual Spanish-speaking, first-generation immigrant who attended an evangelical church, it seems probable that his attitudes regarding his daughter's sexuality would be fairly conservative. Norma, however, was open about her sexuality with family and friends.[19] And although she attended inner-city Johnston High School, the school also housed the district's Liberal Arts Academy magnet program, where Norma would have had extracurricular and elec-

---

[19] According to media reports, Norma was open about her sexuality with family and friends.

tive classes with students from all over Austin, many of which were openly gay.[20]

In this case, public policy in Texas would have been on the side of Norma's individual right to express her sexual orientation. The Texas anti-sodomy law had been repealed by the U.S. Supreme Court in 2003, and a state hate crimes statute including sexual orientation was signed into law in 2001. There were no specific policies that would have established a minority group's right to deny one of its adult members the right to express their sexual orientation. Without any official policy allowing him to deny his adult daughter the right to enter a lesbian relationship, Aviles may have committed what has been termed a "reactive" hate crime. Reactive hate crimes, one of the most common forms, are ones in which "perpetrators attack to protect their turf and resources from the intrusion of unwelcome

---

[20] This analysis is primarily from my personal experience as a teacher in both the Johnston neighborhood program as well as the magnet program.

outsiders."[21] Aviles may have seen himself as protecting his daughter from encroachment by an outsider, Norma, whose individual rights to her sexuality were legally protected by state and federal law.

LGBT Civil Rights in the U.S.

The modern LGBT movement at the time of the Hurtado murders in 2011 was focused on securing equal rights under the law for LGBT persons and has made tremendous gains in that regard. According to LGBT organizer and attorney Urvashi Vaid in her 2012 book *Irresistible Revolution: Confronting Race, Class and the Assumptions of LGBT Politics*, "For the LGBT movement today, equality means the formal recognition of LGBT people in all legal codes, equal access to all institutions and systems in society, and equal

---

[21] Dancygier, Rafaela and Donald P. Green. "Hate Crimes" from *The SAGE Handbook of Prejudice, Stereotyping, and Discrimination*. Sage Press, 2010.

protection under one standard of law."[22] This has resulted in a focus on issues such as marriage equality, workplace non-discrimination, repeal of the U.S. Military's DADT policy, and hate crime laws. To the extent that a movement towards equal rights for LGBT persons also changes cultural attitudes, norms, and incentives, these policies can certainly go a long way to reducing both violent and non-violent acts.

However, Vaid cites two limitations of this approach. First, the broadening of civil and legal rights often does not lead to changed societal norms and attitudes towards the minority group. And secondly, the expansion of these rights is largely insufficient to address racial and economic inequities.[23] For example, while legal barriers for women and minorities were largely removed during the civil rights and feminist movements in the United States, ingrained institutional and

---

[22] Vaid, Urvashi. *Irresistible Revolution: Confronting Race, Class, and the Assumptions of LGBT Politics* p 8. Magnus Books: New York 2012.

[23] Vaid, Chapter 2.

cultural prejudices remained, and issues of socioeconomic inequality and injustice persist. This is especially the case among the most marginalized members of these groups.

An Alternative Approach — The Role of Race, Class, Gender, and Family Structure.

Categorical Inequality and Intersectionality

In his 2007 book *Categorically Unequal*, Princeton sociologist Doug Massey outlines the mechanisms which have produced a marked increase in income inequality and racial and gender stratification in the United States since 1972. According to Massey's framework, stratification develops within three interrelated categories: race, class, and gender. With respect to race, notwithstanding historic civil rights legislation during the 1960s, the wage gap between African Americans and white Americans has not diminished. Similarly, the Hispanic-white wage differential has not only persisted during this time but has widened.[24] In terms of class stratification, there has been a drastic increase in income inequality since 1972 between the wealthiest and poorest Americans, wiping out all gains made since the Great Depression to reduce inequality and build a vibrant middle class.[25]

With respect to gender, while the feminist movement has led to increased opportunities for women in the workplace and the male-female wage differential has closed somewhat, much of the gain is due to stagnant male wages. The women who have gained access to skilled jobs with at least some income parity with men have been mostly educated white women. Conversely, minority women are among the lowest wage earners today due to lower levels of education, continued racial discrimination, and an increase in single-parent households among minorities.[26] Massey claims that these three categories: race,

---

[24] Massey, Doug. *Categorically Unequal*, Chapter 2 pages 51-113. Russell Sage Foundation: New York, 2007.

[25] Massey Chapter 4, pages 113-158.

[26] Massey Chapter 5, pages 158-211.

class, and gender have interacted to produce some of the highest levels of inequality and stratification our country has ever seen.

In his 2010 book *Strangers in a Strange Land*,[27] Massey reiterates this framework with one change: he places gender within a new category, "family structure", as the third leg in the stratification formula: race, class, and family structure. In this context, the notion of family structure includes traditional nuclear families, extended families, as well as non-traditional families of choice. My central claim is that this broader framework of race, class, gender, and family structure is a much more useful context in which to assess and address the issues affecting LGBT persons today, and the Hurtado murders in particular.

What constitutes much of the LGBT rights agenda could be fit into these different categories. Marriage equality, adoption, and visitation rights would be part of the "family structure" category.

---

[27] Massey, Doug. *Strangers in a Strange Land.* W.W. Norton and Company: New York. 2005.

Employment and housing non-discrimination are factors that impact one's economic class. In this context, issues within the traditional LGBT equal rights agenda can be seen as independent variables which impact much broader categories and outcomes for the LGBT community as a result of socioeconomic, racial, gender, and familial stratification. With this approach in mind, I will analyze the Hurtado murders first with respect to the victim, and then the perpetrator.

The Victims

I will focus on Norma Hurtado, the primary target in the murders. Norma was an openly gay, working-class, Hispanic woman who lived in one of the poorest neighborhoods in Austin. She met her partner Lidia at a Dove Springs Wendy's where they both worked. In their book *Place Matters*, Dreier, Mollenkopf, and Swanstron describe how the increased segregation of income groups into distinct geographic locales accentuates a bifurcation in society through unequal access to schools, parks, jobs, medical services, and safety.[28] Dove Springs is on the losing end of this formulation.

Austin as a whole, on the other hand, has the highest median income and highest per-capita property values in the state. It is the state capital, home of the University of Texas, and has a vibrant high-tech, knowledge-based economy. Richard Florida attributes Austin's high-tech success to its ability to attract a high-skilled, highly creative workforce in large part because of its open attitudes towards gays, lesbians, artists, and other members of "the creative class".[29] On the other hand, Austin has one of the highest levels of income inequality in the country, and its poverty and child poverty rates are both higher than the

---

[28] Dreier, Peter, John Mollenkopf and Todd Swanstrom, *Place Matters*. University Press of Kansas. 2004.

[29] Florida, Richard. *Rise of the Creative Class*. Basic Books: New York City 2002.

state and national average, and follow the pattern of racial stratification Massey outlines above.[30]

Norma Hurtado would also have experienced this economic and cultural bifurcation acutely as a student at Johnston High School where I taught her. Johnston served both the low-income, minority Dove Springs student population as well as a district magnet program with a much more affluent and culturally/politically liberal student population in which being "out" was more socially acceptable. Compounding these challenges was the district's "Diversity Choice" policy which allowed minority students to transfer to more successful high schools within the district. Over 50% of students living in the Johnston attendance zone transferred, most of whom were middle class and/or high-performing minority students from the east side of Austin, leaving behind a student population that came from families that were predominantly poor, single-

---

[30] Castillo, Juan. "School age poverty rose in Austin after 2007, but some areas fare better than others", *Austin-American Statesman* article, December 16, 2012.

parent, and immigrant. Therefore, on one hand, Norma would have been exposed to more openly gay peers and role models as a result of the district's magnet program policy, while at the same time, she was relegated to one of the most academically troubled schools in the state, with little chance for upward mobility or the capacity to leave Dove Springs.

This example is reflective of a larger context Norma lived in. On one hand, she lived in a socially progressive metropolitan area which may have given her the courage to live her life openly as a lesbian. Norma was proudly "out" as an adult as well as to her peers in high school. At the same time as a Latina, immigrant, working-class woman she was bound to one of the poorest and least safe neighborhoods in a city marked by racial and economic stratification.

The Perpetrator

José Aviles, like Norma, was Latino, working class, and lived in Dove Springs. He also was an immigrant and monolingual Spanish speaker. At the time of the murders his daughter was eighteen, had a three-year-old child of her own, and had been dating Norma for at least a year. The two families lived within a mile of each other and according to police reports had been fighting for several months. Aviles had sent death threats to Norma via text message, warning her to stop seeing his daughter.[31]

A 2010 review of literature on hate crimes by Rafaela Dancygier and Donald P. Green outlines the individual and contextual accounts of perpetrator motivations. Social, economic, and political factors may help to explain Aviles' motivation in the Hurtado murders. One factor is the influence of small group and community norms.[32] It could be that within Aviles' immediate immigrant community and his evangelical congregation, homosexuality was condemned, and therefore a relationship with Norma was seen as a threat to his daughter's moral integrity.

---

[31] Grisales, Claudia, "Police: Dad Shot Two Women Over Daughter's Relationship", *Austin-American Statesman* article, April 19th, 2011.

[32] Dancygier, p. 300.

Another motivating factor in hate crimes may be the rise of a minority group's political power.[33] In this case, the LGBT community would be the minority community that had made tremendous gains in relative political power within the years immediately preceding the Hurtado Murders, both within Austin and nationally. Aviles also belonged to a minority community, so for this reasoning to hold he would have to perceive a relative loss of power as a result. Also, a 2005 study demonstrated an increase in a city's hate crimes based on sexual orientation, as the city's gender inequality decreased.[34] It is worth noting that at least two other assaults on LGBT persons in Austin occurred in February 2010 and September 2012.

A third possible motivation for hate crimes is a perceived threat as a result of economic and technological changes as a result of globalization.[35] Aviles was an undocumented immigrant

---

[33] Dancygier, p. 301.

[34] Dancygier, p. 303.

[35] Dancygier, p. 302.

living in a poor neighborhood within a wealthy city with a dynamic economy. Austin has a high rate of immigration of both high-skilled tech workers from across the country and the world, and lower-skilled Latin American immi-grants working in the service and construction sectors. It is possible that Aviles felt the pressure of this social and economic change acutely, and it might have been easier to displace this anxiety on a "scapegoat", namely Norma.

It seems that a mix of these factors would have contributed to Aviles' murder of Norma and Maria Hurtado: religious-based homophobia, a perceived loss of power from a male in a culturally traditional family structure in the face of changing cultural norms on sexuality and gender equality, and the impact of economic marginalization in a rapidly changing economic and social landscape. Other factors like Aviles' psychological condition would have to be assessed, but the hate crimes research outlined here points to this inter-connected set of factors.

Closing

José Aviles was undoubtedly motivated by homophobia and a strong bias against Norma Hurtado, his daughter's romantic partner. This bias was obviously based on Norma's sexual orientation. The point of this analysis is not to deny that this hate crime was motivated by anti-gay bias, but to better understand how the issues of race and class interact with attitudes towards sexuality and family structure and lead to this type of conflict and violence. To fully understand the factors that contributed to these murders, I believe it is necessary to see this case through a broader lens than the modern LGBT rights framework. Rather, the fight for legal rights for LGBT persons is best understood as part of a broader set of issues that affect the lives of LGBT persons: namely race, class, and family structure. Public policy which addresses inequities within and across these categories could have a strong impact on the lives of LGBT persons generally and play a role in preventing tragedies like the murder of Norma and Maria Hurtado.

Chapter 3

A Broader Lens from the International Stage: The Development of International LGBT Rights as Part of the Human Rights Movement

Sometimes we need to break the paradigm we are operating in. For example, many of the early gay rights activists in the United States in the 1950s and 1960s patterned their tactics and messaging after the Black civil rights movement. At the same time, early attempts to integrate people of color into the mainstream gay rights movement in organizations like the Mattachine Society were unsuccessful. People of color charted their own course and led the Stonewall Riots and later LGBT rights organizations.

Similarly, to move beyond the traditional "legal rights" framework of the US-based LGBT rights movement, we need to see LGBT rights first as human rights, in the broadest scope of civil, economic, health, political, gender, and religious rights best understood in the international human rights framework. Preventing anti-LGBT hate crimes like the Hurtado murders requires understanding the range of disparities that Norma faced in her everyday life as a Latina lesbian immigrant in a low-income neighborhood like Dove Springs. This chapter charts the development of international LGBT rights as part of the international human rights movement and US foreign policy, and highlights some of the impressive work of activists, NGOs, and government officials. I also explore the more recent movement towards an intersectional approach in the US-based LGBT movement through my personal organizing experience with a statewide LGBT rights organization after same-sex marriage became legalized.

Context

It was not until December of 2011 that the UN issued its first report on the state of international LGBT rights. The report documented that in seventy-six countries, reaching every region of the world, homosexual conduct was still illegal, and in at least five countries was punishable by death. The report finds that in addition to legal imprisonment and capital punishment, LGBT persons are frequently subject to assaults, rapes, kidnappings, and murder.[36] Today the UN officially considers LGBT rights as human rights, and its High Commissioner on Human Rights has called on offending countries to decriminalize homosexual conduct. In the U.S. and Great Britain, foreign aid is now tied, in part, to a recipient country's LGBT rights record. Further, international NGOs like Amnesty International, Human Rights Watch, and the International Gay and Lesbian Human Rights Commission

---

[36] United Nations News Center article, "UN Issues First Report on Human Rights of Gay and Lesbian People." December 15, 2011.

(IGLHRC) conduct detailed country reports and activist campaigns to fight LGBT rights violations internationally.

However, this strong stance by the UN, Western governments, and international NGOs on LGBT rights has developed relatively recently as part of the broader human rights movement. This is partly a result of British colonial legacy, U.S. and British domestic policy towards homosexuals, divisions within the UN, and the particular evolution of the broader agendas of international NGOs. Nevertheless, there has been tremendous progress on international LGBT rights in the past several years.

Legacy of the West

According to a 2006 Human Rights Watch report conducted by then LGBT Program Director Scott Long, more than half of the nearly eighty countries that still criminalized homosexuality did so because of anti-sodomy laws that were put in place by British colonial legislators and jurists. "They brought in the legislation, in fact, because they thought 'native' cultures did not punish 'perverse' sex enough. The colonized needed compulsory re-education in sexual mores."[37] Though the colonizers left, the laws remained in place, remnants of a Victorian, imperial, British culture. HRW called on these countries to repeal these laws as remnants of Western oppression.

In the relatively recent past, it was U.S. and British domestic policy that prevented LGBT rights from becoming a foreign policy priority. Historians Margot Canaday and David Carter chronicled the development of repressive anti-sodomy and anti-homosexual laws at the federal, state, and local level in the U.S. throughout the early to mid-twentieth century. In nearly every U.S. state at some point in the twentieth century persons convicted of homosexual conduct could be fined, imprisoned, institutionalized, or denied employment and citizenship status. The onset of the modern-day gay rights movement did not begin until the late 1960s and it wasn't until 2003,

---

[37] Long, Scott. "This Alien Legacy". A report for Human Rights Watch. Dec. 17, 2008, p. 1.

thirty-four years later, that the Supreme Court overturned U.S. anti-sodomy laws in *Lawrence vs. Texas*.[38] Similarly, British anti-homosexual statutes were instituted in the late nineteenth century and not undone until the late 1960s.[39] Given the U.S. and British role in the creation and growth of the UN, it is not surprising that LGBT rights did not become part of UN human rights policy or the foreign policies of either of these nations until relatively recently. To put this evolution in context, however, it is necessary to start with a brief overview of the development of the international human rights movement more generally.

---

[38] Canday, Margot. *The Straight State*. (Princeton: Princeton University Press, 2009), pp. 1-16.

Carter, David. *Stonewall*. (New York: St. Martin's Press) p. 15.

[39] Houlbrook, Matt. *Queer London* (Chicago: University of Chicago Press, 2005). Chapter 1.

International Human Rights

The fact that the international LGBT rights
movement grew out of the human rights movement, as opposed to the U.S. gay rights
movement, is key to understanding its nature
today. The gay rights movement in the United
States had traditionally been based on civil rights,
and in particular equal protection under the law,
and not directly with economic, cultural, and
social rights. [40]

The international human rights movement can
trace its lineage back to documents that focus on
civil and political rights like the U.S. Declaration
of Independence and the French Declaration of
the Rights of Man and Citizen. [41] However, the
post-World War II human rights movement was
grounded in a much broader set of rights from the
beginning. F.D.R's articulation of the "Four

---

[40] Vaid, Urvashi, *The Irresistible Revolution.* (New York:
Magnus Books, 2012).

[41] Sikkink, Kathryn. *Mixed Signals: U.S. Human Rights
Policy and Latin America* (Cornell: Cornell University Press,
2004), p. 5.

Freedoms" counted political expression, religion, and economic and physical security as basic human rights.[42] After the adoption of the Universal Declaration of Human Rights in 1948, two documents were developed: the "Covenant on Civil and Political Rights" and "Covenant on Economic, Social, and Cultural Rights".[43] Both were eventually proposed in 1954 and adopted in 1966, and the international human rights movement has largely kept this broad scope since.

Both the Cold War and U.S. Southern racism constrained the U.S.'s participation in the international human rights movement through much of the 1950s and 1960s. Support continued to grow, however, in Europe and Latin America where its roots had been strong from the beginning.[44] As Kathryn Sikkink argues, U.S. interest in human rights expanded in the 1970s, first in Congress and eventually in the Carter White House. It was also an issue that united the

---

[42] Ibid., p. 2.

[43] Ibid., p. 36.

[44] Ibid.

conservative and liberal wings of the Democratic Party.[45] Human rights as a framework for U.S. foreign policy has ebbed and flowed through successive U.S. administrations, but nevertheless, institutional mechanisms for monitoring and sanctioning human rights violators remained in place.

LGBT Rights Emerging as
Part of Human Rights Agenda

Local Activism and International Aid

LGBT issues began to emerge on the international stage in the 1990s, but not always as part of the traditional human rights framework. According to Kyle Knight, International Public Policy Fellow at the LGBT-focused Williams Institute at UCLA Law School, it was U.S. and UN funding for HIV and AIDS work internationally that became seed money and eventually ongoing funding for LGBT activist and advocacy groups in the developing

---

[45] Ibid., p. 74

world. "Starting in the 1990s as HIV funding poured into the developing world, human rights work around LGBT issues came out."[46]

Framing LGBT rights within a public health paradigm rather than as part of a human rights framework often provided more cover for activists in these countries. According to Knight, who was writing a book on the LGBT rights movement in Nepal, many LGBT rights groups are still registered as HIV/AIDS prevention groups. LGBT activists in these countries have been hesitant to break from this model since the large amounts of money pouring in have strengthened the LGBT movement over time. Also, in the 1990s most people working at the UN in New York and Geneva were involved with LGBT rights through their larger work with HIV/AIDS.[47]

---

[46] Conversation with Kyle Knight on May 9th, 2013. Mr. Knight is currently in Nepal on a Fulbright Scholarship writing a book on the LGBT rights movement there.

[47] Ibid.

International NGO's and LGBT Rights

While HIV/AIDS funding provided a lifeline to local activist organizations in developing countries, international NGOs became involved in LGBT rights through the human rights movement. The first major organization was the International Gay and Lesbian Human Rights Commission (IGLHRC), formed by U.S. activist Julie Dorf in 1990. After some early victories on asylum cases, IGLHRC secured the commitment of the U.S. State Department to include abuse towards LGBT persons in their yearly country reports.[48] Throughout the 1990s IGLHRC was the primary group working on LGBT rights internationally, expanding its work across Africa, Latin America, and Asia. During this period IGLHRC expanded its training, monitoring, and legal networks.[49]

Starting in the late 1990s an interesting relationship between IGHRC and Human Rights

---

[48] IGLHRC Website: www.iglhrc.org.

[49] Ibid.

Watch developed. What started as IGLHRC simply renting a cubicle at HRW in New York so one of its staff could plan their annual awards dinner, eventually evolved into IGLHRC Program Director Scott Long being permanently located in the HRW office. According to American University Law Professor Julie Mertus in her account of the evolution of international LGBT work by NGOs, this arrangement helped open HRW's awareness on the issue of LGBT rights. Then in 2003, Long left IGLHRC to establish the LGBT Rights Program at the Human Rights Watch. This marked the first time a major international human rights organization with a broad agenda established a permanent LGBT rights program.[50] According to Mertus, "Almost immediately after he took the new post in 2003, Long remembers, his abilities to exert influence in international human rights circles had increased

---

[50] Mertus, Julie. "Applying the Gatekeeper Model of Human Rights Activism: The U.S. Based Movement for LGBT Rights." *In The International Struggle for New Human Rights.* Ed. Clifford Bob (Philadelphia: University of Pennsylvania Press).

substantially."[51] Over the next several years, Long built the HRW program into one of the world's most prominent LGBT rights operations.

Amnesty International actually became involved in LGBT issues earlier than HRW. In this case, it was the result of direct agitation from within its own membership. Founded primarily as a membership organization focused on prisoner-of-conscience issues, by the early 1990s AI had developed into a complex, international organization with an intricate governing system of groups, sections, and members, and focused on broad human rights agendas.[52]

During the 1980s there was objection within the organization to addressing LGBT issues because they did not fit the "prisoner of conscience" (POC) model. There were also concerns about criticizing countries where homosexual activity was illegal, but that otherwise accepted broader human rights mandates. After continued internal agitation by

---

[51] Ibid., p. 59.

[52] Ibid., p. 54.

members as well as external pressure from
IGLHRC, AI in 1991 finally included LGBT
persons within its POC mandate. In 1994, AI
became the first international organization to
produce a monograph on LGBT rights as human
rights, and in 2001 released its first report on the
abuse and torture of LGBT persons.[53] Like HRW,
over the past decade Amnesty International has
been a leader on LGBT rights on the world stage.

The changes at both HRW and AI towards the
inclusion of LGBT rights were not mutually
exclusive. In fact, Mertus argues that one factor
that pushed HRW to begin addressing LGBT
issues was AI's increasing involvement, and in
particular its 1994 report "Breaking the Silence".
Both groups were also influenced by expanded
interest and energy in the human rights
movement after the fall of the Soviet Union, and
in particular the proliferation of international
human rights conferences during this time.[54] By
the early to mid-2000s, IGLHRC, HRW, and AI all

---

[53] Ibid., p. 56.

[54] Ibid.

had vibrant and highly visible programs to address LGBT rights.

The UN and U.S. Foreign Policy

In 1993, the U.N. created the position of U.N. High Commissioner for Human Rights. Also, during the 1990s, there was a dramatic increase in human rights field operations, which included "monitoring human rights violations, education, training, and other advisory services.[55] Couching LGBT rights within the human rights framework, however, brought with it liabilities, namely the charge from many African and Middle Eastern nations that these issues simply didn't fit within accepted norms of human rights. While the U.N. is split largely by continent on the issue, a majority has emerged in recent years in support of international LGBT rights.

---

[55] "Human Rights and the United Nations." United Nations Website: https://www.un.org/cyberschoolbus/humanrights/about/history.asp.

Boris Dittrich, now a member of the Dutch Senate, was the Director of Advocacy for LGBT Rights for the Human Rights Watch from 2007 to 2018. Before that, Dittrich was a member of the Dutch Parliament and part of the successful effort to make the Netherlands the first country to recognize civil unions. While he says organizations like the Human Rights Watch had begun to notice the harsh and often brutal treatment of LGBT persons globally for a number of years, for Mr. Dittrich the pivotal moment was the passage of a landmark document in 2006, the Yogyakarta Principles.[56]

Named after the city in Indonesia where a group of international human rights experts and advocates met in 2006, the Yogyakarta Principals are the first major attempt to systematically apply universal human rights standards to LGBT issues in an international context. The group drafting the principals included representatives from the International Commission of Jurists, UN officials,

---

[56] Much of this background comes from a telephone conversation I had with Mr. Dittrich on May 8, 2013.

academics, and members of NGOs and treaty bodies.[57] The principals are grounded in what the signatories consider binding legal standards enforceable within the context of human rights law.

The principles include: "extrajudicial executions, violence and torture, access to justice, privacy, non-discrimination, rights to freedom and expression and assembly, employment, health, education, immigration and refugee issues, public participation, and a variety of other rights."[58] While the signatories state that states are ultimately responsible for the implementation of the principles, it is clear the document was developed with a central UN role in mind. Individual states would be subject to international pressure, both formal and informal, as well as potential pressure from the media, non-governmental organizations, and national human rights organizations.

---

[57] Website: The Yogyakarta Principals. http://www.yogya kartaprinciples.org/principles_en.htm.

[58] Ibid.

The crucial moment for the United Nations happened in 2008 when for the first time it seriously discussed LGBT rights. In December of that year, a statement was presented to the U.N. General Assembly backed by the European Union and initiated in particular by the French and Dutch. The statement, intended to be adopted as a resolution, but eventually presented as a declaration for lack of support, cites the Yogyakarta Principles and the explicit language which grounded LGBT rights in international human rights law. Noting that homosexual conduct was sanctioned in almost eighty countries, the French Secretary for Human Rights said, "How can we tolerate the fact that people are stoned, hanged, decapitated, and tortured only because of their sexual orientation?"[59]

The declaration received the support of sixty-six countries, with broad support from European and Latin American countries. The United States was not among them. Bush administration

---

[59] Mac Farquhar, Neil. "In a First, Gay Rights are Pushed at the U.N.," *New York Times*, December 19th, 2008.

officials cited a concern for "states' rights", as it had when it refused to sign the Yogyakarta Principles.[60] Further, a block of sixty nations led by the Islamic Conference supported an opposing statement that was read in the General Assembly. This statement claimed that the pro-LGBT efforts undermined current human rights standards by normalizing pedophilia. The Catholic Church also publicly opposed the pro-LGBT declaration. The Islamic Conference failed in a last-minute attempt to alter another resolution by Sweden condemning summary executions, objecting to including "sexual orientation" among the central reasons for these executions.[61]

On March 22nd of 2011, the U.S. issued a declaration, supported by more than eighty U.N. countries, entitled the Joint Statement on Ending Acts of Violence and Related Human Rights Violations Based on Sexual Orientation & Gender

---

[60] Ibid. Conversation with Mr. Dittrich.

[61] Ibid. *New York Times* 12/19/2008.

Identity.[62] This marked the first time the U.S. had taken the lead at the UN on LGBT rights. In December of 2011, U.S. Secretary of State Clinton gave her landmark speech in Geneva declaring that "Gay rights are human rights."[63] Under the Obama administration, the U.S. had also joined the UN Human Rights Council, reversing the Bush Administration decision to withdraw from that body. A few years earlier the Obama administration signed the Yogyakarta Principles, which the Bush administration had refused to endorse.

Another major sea change in LGBT rights at the UN occurred on June 17th, 2011, when the UN Human Rights Council passed a resolution expressing "grave concern" regarding abuses based on sexual orientation and commissioning a global report on LGBT human rights abuses. [64]

---

[62] Donahue, Eileen Chamberlain. U.S. Ambassador to the Human Rights Council at Geneva. Press Release 3/22/11

[63] U.S. Secretary of State Hillary Clinton. Speech on LGBT Rights. December 6, 2001. Palais des Nations, Geneva, Switzerland.

[64] Jordans, Frank. "UN Gay Rights Protection Resolution Passes, Hailed as Historic Moment" *Huffington Post*, 6/17/11.

This was the first time the UN officially categorized LGBT rights as human rights. The declaration was forwarded by South Africa, and backed strongly by Europe, Latin America, and the United States. Countries voting against included Russia, Saudi Arabia, Nigeria, and Pakistan. Boris Dittrich of Human Rights Watch cited South Africa's role as key, since LGBT rights have often been portrayed as an imposition of Western values on Africa and the Middle East.[65] After the vote, Nigeria claimed the declaration was counter to African values.

Movement to a Broader Lens in
Today's U.S. LGBT Rights Movement

Mainstream LGBT organizations have gradually moved over the past several years to a more intersectional approach, largely led by LGBT people of color bringing organizing and advocacy experience from racial and economic justice movements. These leaders have demanded the

---

[65] Ibid.

movement become more responsive to the full set of pressures and inequities that come with multiple systems of oppression. Another reason for this shift has been that many LGBT organizations have taken stock after the 2015 Obergefell ruling and begun to explore their focus in the post-marriage equality phase of the movement.

I worked for Equality California in 2015-2016 just as same-sex marriage was legalized nationwide and two years after it had been legalized in California in 2013. Though a financial supporter and student of the LGBT movement for years, I had spent the previous decade working in broad-based organizing with the Industrial Areas Foundation, the largest and longest-standing network of faith and community-based organizations in the country. The IAF is the best training ground for organizers, and as a broad coalition of primarily religious congregations, we focused on issues such as immigration, workforce development, community safety, and education. This gave me a strong grounding in working with the most marginalized communities in Austin and

San Antonio on a broad range of issues. What it did not give me is a grounding in working on LGBT issues, since our organizations only took on policy issues that our congregations, ranging from Unitarian to Catholic, could agree on.

When I left for graduate school in 2012 after a decade of organizing with the IAF, I was determined to work in the LGBT movement, which at the time was focused on marriage equality. But just after my graduation from Princeton's MPP Program in the Spring of 2013 and my impending move to California to be closer to family, the Supreme Court handed down its decision to overturn the ban on same-sex marriage in California. I landed in the Golden State a day late and a dollar short, just as the movement was moving elsewhere. After another year of graduate school in Los Angeles, I landed a job at Equality California as the Director of Programs and Program Development. The organization had just pivoted from winning over eighty pieces of civil rights of legislation over the past few decades to a broader mission focused on intersectionality and cross-movement organizing.

My primary project aimed at reducing healthcare disparities for LGBT undocumented immigrants in the Central Valley, which is much poorer, more rural, and more conservative than California's coastal areas. While the marriage equality movement had been an adept legal and public education strategy focused on the legal right to marry, the project in the Central Valley actually played more to my experience in organizing around issues like immigration and healthcare, and in a region that was right-of-center politically, similar to Texas. We designed and conducted LGBT cultural competency training for health clinic staff, who were predominantly Latino and under forty. While the content was new material for many of these providers, the discussion of healthcare disparities and the challenges undocumented patients faced was familiar. I organized town halls in Bakersfield and Fresno bringing together LGBT centers, immigration groups, and healthcare clinics and providers.

One of the key concepts we discussed was the negative impact on healthcare disparities when a person belongs to more than one marginalized group, in this case being an undocumented immigrant, LGBT, a person of color, and low-income. Being from any one of these groups leads to negative health outcomes, and being from two or three compounds the challenges.

There were no easy solutions. But grappling with these issues in the Central Valley with all these stakeholders helped me understand intersectionality better than any book I've read or paper I wrote in graduate school. Organizer and civil rights leader Dolores Huerta was on the Equality California board and ran her foundation out of Bakersfield where she was still very involved in local politics. The legendary organizer-leader of the farmworkers was an LGBT advocate since the 1980s. She talked with conviction about the need to organize to undo multiple factors of oppression.

My experience in the Central Valley was not only life-giving but healing. I had always felt as an organizer I hadn't done enough immediately following Norma's death, especially as a gay man. I finally felt I was taking action using all of my organizing skills and all aspects of my identity. It began to break down the compartmentalization in my mind that prevented me from thinking intersectionally and gave me the courage and imagination to act against an injustice that doesn't fit neatly into categories.

Chapter 4

The Importance of Developing an Institutional Strategy for Power and Leadership within the LGBT Rights Movement

This chapter deals with the central role of institutions in the struggle for LGBT rights, both in the development of political leadership, and in the type of political power necessary for a long-term struggle to maintain a seat at the table in American politics. As an organizer with the Industrial Areas Foundation for over 15 years, and as an LGBT person who has studied the gay rights movement, I am attempting to integrate my understanding of broad-based institutional organizing with an identity-based movement, both of which I care deeply about.

At the center of my argument is the importance of civic and religious institutions in the struggle for LGBT rights. Though traditionally some of these institutions have been hostile to LGBT persons, many are now more open and accepting. I believe congregations and civic organizations can have a central role in building the political power and leadership for the ongoing LGBT rights struggle. I will end the chapter with some specific recommendations for the type of organizations that I believe could achieve this.

The Most Important Fight

I am challenged by two passages from Chapter 9 of Hanna Arendt's *Origins of Totalitarianism*:

> "Man, it turns out, can lose all so-called Rights of Man without losing his essential quality as man, his human dignity. Only the loss of a polity itself expels him from humanity."[66]

---

[66] Arendt, Hannah. *The Origins of Totalitarianism*. (New York: Harcourt Books, 1966) p. 297.

"We are not born equal; we become equal as members of a group on the strength of our decision to guarantee ourselves mutually equal rights."[67]

Embedded in the first quote is Arendt's critique of the notion of rights as expressed in "The Declaration of the Rights of Man and the Citizens" which established the notion of human rights as universal, natural, and not tied to any particular political entity or state. For Arendt, "the right to have rights" is supreme, and by that, she means the right to belong to a political community. A political community exists within a specific state, at a specific time, under a governing set of laws that establishes the requirements of citizenship. A political state, and political space established within that state, is not natural or immutable, but rather an artifice, constructed by the work of human hands. For Arendt, this is the stuff of politics, and to be expelled from the polity means to lose the standing and capacity for political action. Outside of the political community, one

---

[67] Ibid p. 301.

cannot fight for other rights such as shelter, food, clothing, education, and other civil rights. Conversely, to possess these basic civil and economic rights, but not to possess the right to participate in politics robs a person of their dignity and capacity for public action. They are human, but not citizens. [68]

In the second passage, Arendt is challenging the enlightenment notion of equality. For Arendt, we are not equal by birth. As humans, we are endowed with different levels of talent, capacity, physical characteristics, and mental capacity. We are defined by our particulars. We can, however, choose to construct a world of durable political institutions in which we are equal as citizens. Humanity is pluralistic, but we literally fabricate a common world in which we choose to endow each other with equality as political persons. It is when this public world is destroyed altogether, or one group is denied or stripped of their right to participate in politics, that they are then exposed to the inequalities of brute existence, unable to

---

[68] Arendt, ibid.

engage in the kind of meaningful action that makes them fully human. This is what happened to the Jews, Arendt claims, under the Nazi regime. Stripped of their rights as citizens, the Jews were expelled and made a stateless people, "unwanted by any political community."[69]

What, if anything, does this have to do with the modern-day struggle for LGBT rights in the United States today? In the U.S., the LGBT community is certainly not in danger of being expelled from society and robbed of citizenship status. Over the past several years the LGBT community has exercised increasingly greater power both within the courts and at the ballot box. The efforts of LGBT organizers and advocates have reaped tremendous gains in the past decade with the repeal of anti-sodomy laws by the U.S. Supreme Court, the federal repeal of the "Don't Ask Don't Tell" policy in the military, the Obergefell decision, and the U.S. Supreme Court's

---

[69] Villa, Dana. *Politics, Philosophy, Terror: Essays on the Thought of Hannah Arendt.* (Princeton: Princeton University Press) p. 38, 1999.

interpretation which applies workplace non-discrimination protections under the 1964 Civil Rights Act to LGBT persons.

Notwithstanding these tremendous gains, I wish to underscore what I believe to be the most important fight for the LGBT community, and any group of citizens for that matter: building the institutional power and leadership necessary to sustain "a place at the table" within American politics. Victories that secured equal access to the institutions of marriage, the military, the workplace, and schools all speak to Arendt's notion of guaranteeing ourselves "mutually equal rights". The prospect remains, however, that these rights are in danger of being taken away if there is not an equally aggressive focus to reclaim a place within the institutions that exert political influence and form leaders with the capacity to practice politics. Many of these institutions are ones in which LGBT persons have traditionally been shut out.

Another reason it is important to see beyond the immediate progress on LGBT rights is the fact that the history of gay rights has not only been progressive, but cyclical as well. While the past decade has seen a generational shift in attitudes toward LGBT people, this progress is always in danger of being rolled back. Gains on marriage equality, the repeal of DADT, and workplace non-discrimination surely mark huge milestones in the struggle for equality under the law, but it would be dangerous to assume that the struggle for LGBT rights will soon be over.

The first half of the twentieth century was one of the most oppressive periods for LGBT persons in the United States. Anti-sodomy laws, official medical diagnoses, and church condemnation branded LGBT persons as criminals, sick, or sinners. According to historian David Carter, "By 1961 the laws in America were harsher on homosexuals than those in Cuba, Russia, or East Germany.... an adult in the privacy of his or her home could get anywhere from a light fine to five, ten, or twenty years — or even life — in prison. In 1971 twenty states had "sex psychopath" laws that permitted the detaining of homosexuals for that reason alone."[70] The situation at the federal level was no better. Princeton historian Margot Canaday writes in her recent book *The Straight State* "From the mid-1940s into the late 1960s the state crafted tools to overtly target homosexuality... policies were enacted that explicitly used homosexuality to define who could enter the country and be naturalized, who could serve in the military, and who could collect state benefits."[71]

Most of the legal restrictions on homosexual behavior and employment that have been undone in the past thirty years were actually instituted within the past century. In many ways, the plight of LGBT persons actually got worse before it got better. Despite an overall move towards progress on LGBT rights, world history gives us examples of retreat as well. Homosexuals, persecuted in Nazi Germany, just a few years earlier had

---

[70] Carter, David. Stonewall: *The Riots that Sparked the Gay Revolution.* (New York: St. Martin's Press, 2004) p. 15.

[71] Canaday, Margo. *The Straight State* (Princeton: Princeton University Press, 2009) p. 3.

enjoyed one of the most open and accepting societies during the Weimar Republic. While the push for LGBT equal rights currently should continue unabated, I believe there should be just as aggressive an effort to build the type of long-term institutional power and leadership necessary to counteract interests that would seek to roll back this progress.

An Institutional Power Analysis
of Modern LGBT Rights History[72]

The pressures that weighed on the LGBT community in the middle of the twentieth century were institutional in nature: government, medical organizations, and the church. The history of the

---

[72] This is primarily my brief analysis of LGBT rights history, with an emphasis on institutional power. I draw heavily from several excellent histories of the LGBT movement including: Randy Shilts "The Mayor of Castro Street" and "The Band Played On," David Carter "Stonewall," Linda Hirschman "Victory," Martin Duberman "Stonewall," David Eisenbach "Gay Power," and Urvashi Vaid "The Irreversible Revolution."

struggle for LGBT rights since then can be told as a struggle of institutions pushing back against the forces of oppression as well.

To underscore the importance of institutions in developing power and leadership for LGBT persons today, I will do a brief analysis of the role of institutions in the struggle for LGBT rights. It is meant to be suggestive rather than exhaustive.

From the onset of the modern-day gay rights struggle through the late 1970s the three most important institutions in the struggle for LGBT rights have been gay and lesbian political organizations, gay and lesbian bars, and LGBT periodicals and publications. These were among the few institutions where LGBT leaders had a voice, could congregate openly, and could exert some political influence. Political organizations that formed through the 1950s through the 1970s included the Mattachine Society, Daughters of Bilitis, ECHO, the Gay Liberation Front, Gay Activists Alliance, and The Council on Religion and the Homosexual.[73] Early LGBT publications included *The Ladder*, *The Mattachine Review*, *ONE*, *The Hymnal*, and *The Advocate*.[74] Gay bars have a crucial role in early gay rights history starting with Jose Sarria's Tavern Guild in 1960's San Francisco, the Stonewall Riots in New York in 1969, and Harvey Milk's use of San Francisco gay bars to support the Teamsters' boycott of Coors beer in the late 1970s.[75]

In the 1980s the AIDS crisis hit, and the Reagan administration and the rise of the religious right provided added pressure on the LGBT community. As a response, new political and service organizations were created, including the Gay Men's Health Crisis, ACT UP, local AIDS health and service organizations, hospices, and

---

[73] Eisenberg, David. *Gay Power: An American Revolution* (New York: Carrol and Graff, 2006).

Shilts, Randy *The Mayor of Castro Street* (New York: St. Martin's Press, 1982).

[74] Eisenberg, Carter, Shilts, Duberman, Martin. *Stonewall.* (New York: Penguin Books, 1994).

[75] Ibid.

charitable foundations. Cultural and entertainment institutions began to have a tremendous impact.[76] Plays like Larry Kramer's *The Normal Heart* and *Angels in America* sought to interpret the AIDS crisis and Reagan conservatism. The latter may have been the most powerful cultural text of the 1990s, winning both the Pulitzer Prize and Tony Awards, playing for nearly a decade between its Broadway and regional theater runs, and was eventually made into an award-winning HBO film. Also, television shows like *Will and Grace* in the late 1990s contributed to a cultural shift in visibility of LGBT persons. More recently, similar positive portrayals of LGBT persons in media and entertainment institutions have had a key impact in improving cultural attitudes towards the LGBT community.

In a sense, the LGBT movement was caught off-guard with the passage of California's Proposition 8, which banned same-sex marriage in 2008 in the state. The pro-Proposition 8 campaign received generous funding from the

---

[76] Ibid.

Mormon church, and targeted members of theologically conservative religious denominations, especially minorities within evangelical, Catholic, and African American churches. The anti-Proposition 8 voter mobilization effort has been critiqued for its ineffectiveness in reaching these same churches and minority populations. In a sense, the anti-marriage forces had a stronger institutional strategy.[77]

However, over the past thirty years, national organizations such as the National Gay and Lesbian Task Force, the Human Rights Campaign, Lambda Legal, Freedom to Marry, and a host of statewide LGBT organizations like Equality California had built an increasingly successful legislative and legal strategy for increasing LGBT rights.[78] The passage of Proposition 8 became one rallying point for LGBT organizations to intensify efforts to overturn same-sex marriage bans at the

---

[77] Cilliza, Chris and Sean Sullivan, "How Proposition 8 Passed in California and Why it Wouldn't Today" (Washingtonpost.com, 3/26/2013).

[78] Vaid, Urvashi. *The Irresistible Revolution*. (New York: Magnum Books, 2012).

state and eventually federal level over the next several years. Another rallying point, as I argue, are the spate of high-profile LGBT deaths by suicide in 2010, and then the record number of anti-LGBT murders in 2011, which included the murders of Norma and Maria Hurtado. The particularly brutal years from 2008-2011 for the LGBT movement provided the anger, energy, and imagination to dramatically shift public opinion that in large part led to the subsequent monumental victories for LGBT equality.

Role of Institutions in the Development of Leaders

Nearly everything I have learned about the importance of institutions and their role in politics and leadership development comes from my experience as an organizer and leader with the Industrial Areas Foundation from the late 1990s through 2012. My attempt to think through the question of political space, leadership, and what is at stake in LGBT politics is an attempt to apply this framework to my experience as a gay man trying to add something to the conversation regarding the LGBT movement and politics.

In the early 1970s, Ernesto Cortes Jr. organized what is now the oldest and most successful community-based political organization in the country, Communities Organized for Public Service, or COPS, in San Antonio, Texas. Professor Jeffrey Stout of Princeton chronicles modern-day IAF broad-based organizing in his recent book, *Blessed Are the Organized*.[79] Stout describes possibly the most significant innovation in grassroots organizing in the past forty years: the way in which Cortes and COPS leaders took the neighborhood-based, community-organizing model established by Saul Alinsky in the 1940s-1960s and transformed it into what is now known as broad-based organizing. The IAF now has sixty organizations nationally, of which COPS is the oldest.

Central to this new model was the importance and role of institutions. Three primary

---

[79] Stout, Jeffrey. *Blessed Are the Organized: Grassroots Democracy in America* (Princeton: Princeton University Press, 2010).

innovations occurred.[80] First, leadership in the former "community organizing" model was taken from local institutions like churches, often robbing them of vital leadership and talent that sustained these institutions. The new "broad-based organizing" model, however, sought to build and strengthen the institution's leadership base first. The goal in broad-based organizing is to build leadership first for the member institution, with the understanding that some of those leaders would participate in the larger collective of the organization. This ethic carries over today. When I was organizing with Austin Interfaith, our leaders had a rule that to be an Austin Interfaith leader, you had to be a leader in good standing within your own congregation, school, or union.

Secondly, in the early days of COPS, a "theology of organizing" was developed with

---

[80] My knowledge of the history of the IAF comes from my experience as an IAF organizer, and specifically in working with the organizers and leaders involved in the development of the modern-day IAF over the past forty years, including Mr. Cortes and Sr. Christine Stephens, both IAF National Co-Directors.

local pastors and bishops so that the work reinforced the values and traditions of these religious institutions. In this way, the search for leadership went beyond just the "social justice activists" and attempted to engage church members who were concerned primarily with the mission of their particular congregation. Thirdly, as COPS organizers and leaders saw traditionally cohesive neighborhoods in urban areas start to become much more disconnected as a result of urban migration patterns starting in the 1970s and 1980s, the IAF model of organizing shifted to address this breakdown in networks of relationships in local communities.

Requisite leadership skills had to evolve too. Organizing became just as much a fight to rebuild and reweave a relational culture within and around member institutions as it was a political fight.[81] The work of leaders (and paid organizers), was to do hundreds of one-on-one individual meetings, small group house meetings, and door-

---

[81] Cortes, Ernesto. "Reweaving the Social Fabric". (*Boston Review*, 1994).

to-door relational walks throughout neighbor-hoods. All told, the institutions of the church, and eventually schools and unions, became the gravitational center of organizing in the IAF because of their capacity to develop leadership, reinforce and live out deeply held values, and rebuild thick networks of relationships in the face of an increasingly individualist culture.

In his article "Towards a Democratic Culture" Cortes pins the decline of democratic values on the weakening of mediating institutions, (congregations, schools, labor unions, civic associations) as the place where the habits and practices of citizenship are taught and developed.[82] In a political culture dominated by polarization, big-dollar ad campaigns, polls, and focus groups, Cortes maintains that mediating institutions are one of the few places where citizens can learn perhaps the most important skill in democratic leadership: how to have a conversation. "Yet it is only through these kinds

[82] Cortes, Ernesto. "Towards a Democratic Culture" (*The Kettering Review*: 2012).

of conversations that people develop the capacity to think long-term, to consider something outside of their own experience, to reconsider their own experience, and to develop a larger vision of their neighborhood, their state, or their society. Unfortunately, people don't develop the capacity to have deliberative conversations on their own. These are skills that must be cultivated inside institutions."[83]

Cortes also outlines some of the specific skills a leader develops through political action within institutions. These include what the Greeks called *philia* or political friendships. Unlike private friendships, these are public relationships born out of struggle, debate, argument, and action. A second skill is *phronesis*, or "practical wisdom", which is again born out of experience, and rooted in tacit knowledge. Finally, leaders learn the value of *praxis* or action which is calculated and reflected upon. This is where leaders learn through successes and mistakes. Certainly, it is possible to learn these leadership skills outside of

---

[83] Ibid, p. 47.

institutions, but institutions provide a unique context for learning democratic citizenship because of their power and capacity for action, their rootedness in tradition and values, and their store of potential talent.[84]

In describing how institutions create the space for conversation and democratic citizenship, Cortes draws from Alexis de Tocqueville's observations of civic and political life in America. In his book *The Fragility of Freedom*, Joshua Mitchell talks about the moderating influence of institutions. He claims that writers such as Tocqueville, Augustine, Hobbes, and Rousseau believed that humans are by nature, immoderate. Specifically, he defines the Augustinian self as "the kind of self that is prone to move in two opposite directions: either inward, in which case it tends to get wholly shut up within itself and abandon the world; or outward, in which case it tends to be restive, overly active, and lost amid the world, searching at a frenzied pace for satisfaction

---

[84] Ibid. p. 48.

it can never find there."[85] According to Mitchell, Tocqueville, in particular, believed participation in institutions helps mitigate these dual inclinations. Tocqueville argued that Americans' inclination towards excessive motion was checked by the moderating influence of church and family, while their inclination to withdraw was counteracted by local political and associational life.[86]

In his book *Public Freedom*, Dana Villa critiques modern-day voices who reduce Tocqueville as simply a champion of volunteerism and associational life, without understanding the political nature of his analysis. This misinterpretation, Villa believes, leads to a notion of civic participation devoid of politics, which misses Tocqueville's point. "Rather, Tocqueville's unique contribution to the "discourse of civil society" is to be found in his remarkable re-visioning of public-political life as dispersed over a non-state terrain. It is in the realm of 'perma-

---

[85] Mitchell, Joshua. *The Fragility of Freedom* (Chicago University Press: Chicago, 1995) p. 3.

[86] Ibid.

nent,' political, and civil associations that citizenship is learned, self-government effected, and debate and argument suffused throughout society."[87] Tocqueville's notion of associational life extends beyond the voluntary sector of congregations and benevolent groups but also includes townships, municipalities, and the free press. What these institutions share is that they are local in nature and have the capacity to help citizens mediate between individual interests and the common interest of the state. Local, political participation develops citizens. "He (Tocqueville) could not help but view American civil society as a seedbed for civic virtue and the 'habit of association' (the forces opposed to individualism), as well as providing the actual space for (decentralized) political participation."[88]

Catholic theologian and political philosopher Robert Sokolowsky argues that civic and religious institutions, while not political institutions in

---

[87] Villa, Dana. *Public Freedom*. (Princeton: Princeton University Press, 2008) p. 45.

[88] Villa, Dana. p. 45.

themselves (in fact he calls them pre-political), nevertheless prepare the human person for political life in a democratic republic. "The Republic presupposes pre-political societies. It does not claim to fabricate men or make men human. It assumes that families and neighborhoods, families and private associations, can all do their irreplaceable work in forming human beings."[89] Sokolowsky, citing Aristotle, claims that before we are formed as citizens and leaders, we need to be formed as human beings. This is the role of civic and religious institutions.

Similarly, Stanley Hauerwas, possibly the most influential Protestant theologian of the past thirty years,[90] believes religious congregations form character and virtue by reinforcing a set of habits and practices in the context of a living community. Hauerwas, who critiques both liberal Protestantism and Christian fundamentalism for

---

[89] Sokolowsky, Robert "The Human Person and Political Life (*The Thomist*, vol. 65,2001) p. 523.

[90] Stout, Jeffrey. *Democracy and Tradition* (Princeton University Press: 2004).

mirroring partisan political lines, sees the role of the church as to form a people who can speak truthfully. In their book *Resident Aliens*, William Willimon and Hauerwas write, "Our project is to recover a sense of adventure by helping the church recover what it means to be a truthful people — a hope American liberals and conservatives have equally abandoned. By 'people' we mean to indicate that the challenge facing the church is political, social, ecclesial - the formation of a visible body of people who know the cost of discipleship and are willing to pay."[91] Taking a step beyond Sokolowsky, Hauerwas sees the role of the church as political, but the process of formation within a community provides its members with the imagination and courage to engage in politics around the church's values.

Hugh Heclo argues in his book *On Thinking Institutionally*, that an openness to institutions allows leaders to see the world from the "inside

---

[91] Hauerwas, Stanley and William Willimon, *Resident Aliens*, (Nashville: Abingdon Press 1989) p. 157.

out."[92] To start, institutions equip leaders with the capacity for "faithful reception", or an openness and inclination to see ourselves as the receptors of a tradition and debtors to those who have given us a world "charged with meaning".[93] Secondly, institutions "infuse value" in the relationships and traditions that constitute them. "These intrinsic values imply relations of obligation, not calculations of convenience or personal preference."[94] Finally, institutions stretch a leader's time horizons. "To think institutionally is to stretch your time horizon backwards and forwards so that the shadows from the past and future lengthen into the present."[95]

Taken together, Heclo's characteristics of institutional thinking suggest that institutions bind us to a larger set of traditions and relationships and deepen our connection to a world that

---

[92] Heclo, Hugh. *On Thinking Institutionally* (East Boulder: Paradigm Press 1982). p 82.

[93] Ibid, p. 98.

[94] Ibid, p. 102.

[95] Ibid, p. 109.

we have an obligation to improve. The African American civil rights movement was largely rooted in the networks, power, and moral traditions of the African American church. The progressive movement was rooted in civic and benevolent organizations like settlement houses, temperance societies, and labor unions. The populist movement was rooted in local agrarian groups like the Farmer's Alliances and Grange Organizations. Beyond providing a network of organized people, religious and civic organizations grounded these movements in local traditions and made them accountable to the people they represented.

The long-term political effectiveness of the LGBT rights movement will partly depend on its capacity to root the struggle in religious and civic institutions. This is not without precedent in LGBT rights history. In the early 1960s, the Council for Religion and the Homosexual (CRE) played a pivotal role in standing with the gay community against police harassment in San

Francisco.[96] Another example is Craig Rodwell, a
key figure in the Stonewall Riots, who carried
with him a zeal for justice and human dignity that
he learned from a devout Christian Science
upbringing. In fact, he opened the first LGBT non-
pornographic bookstore and community center in
the United States. It was modeled after Christian
Science Reading Rooms, and eventually became
the center of his political organizing during and
after Stonewall.[97] More recently, religious leaders
like New Hampshire Episcopal Bishop Gene
Robinson and Conservative Jewish Rabbi Elliot
Dorff of Los Angeles have worked tirelessly for
justice and acceptance of LGBT people within
their denominations.

Recommendations and Closing

Certainly, national and statewide LGBT groups
have achieved remarkable success over the past
decade. Further, the culture, entertainment, and

---

[96] Shilts, *The Mayor of Castro Street*.

[97] Carter, ibid.

advertising industries increasingly are catering to the purchasing power of the LGBT community. On the other hand, it was only in the past few decades that Proposition 8 passed in perhaps the most liberal state in the country, thirty states banned same-sex marriage, and a spate of teen suicides and hate crimes brought LGBT issues into the national consciousness. Often the sources of oppression are local in nature, whether at a school where bullying is permitted, a church that condemns homosexuality, or an unaccepting family. The best political response should be very local in nature too, rooted in the institutions of local communities and focused on building local leadership.

I believe there is a need for metropolitan, institutionally based political organizations focused on building leadership and power around issues affecting the LGBT community. These organizations could be coalitions of institutions that serve or are allies of the LGBT community. This could include progressive religious congregations, LGBT service and health organizations, LGBT charitable organizations,

LGBT student and university groups, and possibly LGBT-owned businesses. These organizations should be owned and run by their member institutions, which could pay dues and raise private funding in order to keep independent of government influence.

Leadership development should be central to the mission of these organizations. In fact, it should be the focus. Rather than developing leaders to address issues, these organizations would choose issues and actions in order to develop leadership. Cortes' notion of "praxis" is central: action which is planned, calculated, and reflected upon. This is how leaders learn and grow. Staff should consist of professional organizers, rather than executive directors so that the identification and development of leadership remain the core work. The issues addressed should emerge from the values and traditions of the member institutions, especially the religious congregations and service organizations, which remind the organization to focus on the most vulnerable members of the LGBT community. Actions should start with the very local issues:

policies at school districts, healthcare districts, cities, and counties. This would be similar to the type of local politics that so impressed Tocqueville.

But these organizations would also need to deal soberly with the realities of power. First, they should work in collaboration with other broad-based and issue advocacy organizations in their metropolitan area. Working with other organizations also mitigates tribalism and insularity. This also provides the potential to build the type of power necessary to take on larger issues. Since issues of race, class, and sexuality interact and intersect, developing strategic allies across issue areas is crucial. To the extent that several of these LGBT political organizations exist within a state, legislative issues could be taken on as well.

Obviously, my recommendations and my reading of the modern-day LGBT rights struggle emerges out of the type of organizing I am familiar with. I have incredible respect for the heroic efforts of organizers, advocates, and activists who have been working on LGBT issues for years. My purpose is to determine what I have to add to the conversation and the struggle.

My own growth and development in the IAF makes me particularly loyal to organizing efforts that are primarily about the development of leaders and citizens. One of my mentors in the IAF once told me that for organizers, the real evidence of our work is not the libraries, parks, and schools that get built. Nor is it even the policies we develop or change for the better. The real evidence in the work of organizing is the "living stones" that get built. By that she meant the leaders we help identify, engage, mentor, and develop. Any effort that focuses on the formation of citizen-leaders, and the institutions necessary to sustain them, has a strong chance of enduring success.

Chapter 5

Lessons in Political Organizing from LGBT History: The Leadership of Jose Sarria, Craig Rodwell, and Harvey Milk

Context and Overview

Nearing the 54th anniversary of the Stonewall Riots, the LGBT community continues the work of building an enduring movement, ready to withstand inevitable backslides and pushback from forces opposed to equality. We have been on the winning side of monumental shifts in public opinion, acceptance, and legal victories impacting family and workplace rights. Over the past several years LGBT organizations have begun to address issues of intersectionality, transgender rights, and remaining gaps in non-discrimination laws at the

federal level and in right-of-center states. In order
to build the effective capacity for this broadened
agenda, organizations in the LGBT movement
need to be grounded in political organizations
with a strong institutional base, focused on
developing and cultivating leaders, and pitched
towards a wide set of issues and allies.

A look at the lives of three key figures in LGBT
history in the U.S. gives us insight into the type of
organizing necessary to build such a long-term
effort. José Sarria, the first openly gay person to
run for elected office in the United States,
organized institutions within San Francisco's gay
community to push back against police oppression starting in the 1950s. Craig Rodwell, an early
gay rights activist in New York, developed his
leadership skills through courageous action
during the 1960s to prepare himself for a crucial
role in the Stonewall Riots at the end of that
decade. And Harvey Milk, whose career was
directly and indirectly formed by Sarria and
Rodwell, built a vision and coalition much
broader than the gay community during his brief
but historic tenure in San Francisco politics.

Coming of age at one of the most repressive times for LGBT persons in Western history, these three figures give us not only a model of courageous leadership, but also insight into fundamentals of effective organizing: engaging with community-based institutions, developing leadership through action, and working with a broad set of issues and allies.

Lesson #1: Organize Institutionally — Jose Sarria

Few political organizations leverage a long-term impact without building a strong institutional base. The Democratic Party in urban areas from the New Deal through the early 1970s drew from a base of labor organizations, the immigrant-friendly Catholic Church, and other civic organizations. The Republican Party of the latter half of the same century was a coalition of disparate groups including evangelical churches,

gun-rights organizations, pro-business organizations, and conservative think tanks.[98]

Institutions like religious congregations, civic
organizations, and unions keep a political
organization grounded in the relationships, talent,
and values of local communities.[99] Until the past
few decades, however, LGBT persons were shut
out of open participation in many of these
institutions: shut out individually in the sense of
not having the freedom to be open about their
sexuality; and shut out as an organized group,
unable to leverage power as an interest group
with institutions and within coalitions. In the
second half of the twentieth century, this left only
a handful that could be tapped as an organizing
base. These included gay and lesbian bars, LGBT

---

[98] Hacker, Jacob S. *Off Center.* New Haven and London: Yale
University Press. pp. 115-121.

[99] My understanding and knowledge of institutional, broad-
based organizing comes from my ten years organizing
professionally with the Industrial Areas Foundation in Austin
and San Antonio. This piece is a synthesis of my
understanding of broad-based organizing my reading of
LGBTQ history.

political and service organizations, and gay and lesbian periodicals. This makes the success José Sarria had in building an institutional base for gay rights in local San Francisco politics starting in the 1950s all the more remarkable.

José Sarria, a celebrated drag performer at the Black Cat Lounge in the North Beach section of San Francisco, emerged as the de facto leader of that city's gay community in the late 1950s by organizing to neutralize the frequent and often brutal police raids on gay bars. Police used statutes outlawing cross-dressing and serving homosexuals in bars to arrest, intimidate, and terrorize gays and lesbians. In response, Sarria organized the city's thirty-five gay and lesbian bars into a communications network, one tipping off the others by phone at the first sight of an officer. Historian Randy Shilts called Sarria's crowded Sunday drag show "the first gay news service", where he would announce, in coded language, which establishments were visited by police.[100] During the 1950s, only a few gay news publications existed. Put out by early gay rights organizations, these included *The Ladder* published by Daughters of Bilitis, and *ONE Magazine*, published by ONE, Inc.

In 1961, in response to a particularly ugly mayoral election two years earlier where homosexual vice became a primary issue, Sarria decided to run for the San Francisco Board of Supervisors. This was the first time an openly gay person ran for elected office in the United States, sixteen years before Harvey Milk would win a seat on the same board in 1977. Rather than campaigning, Sarria let the word spread through his network of bars. He shocked the political establishment by garnering over 7,000 votes, placing sixth out of twenty-nine candidates, and for the first time establishing the gay community in San Francisco as a political force.[101]

---

[100] Shilts, Randy. *The Mayor of Castro Street*. New York: St. Martin's Griffin. 1982. (p. 52).

[101] Ibid. pp. 56-57.

Police attempted to destroy Sarria's institutional base after the election, cracking down on gay and lesbian bars across the city until only eighteen remained. The Black Cat, where Sarria performed, closed in 1963. This suppression of the LGBT community occurred as a result of anti-vice politics of the early 1960s in many major cities, and also in the context of the repressive post-war period in which a proliferation of anti-homosexual laws were enacted, including one enacted in 1966 in San Francisco which prohibited men from dressing in women's clothing with an intent to deceive. As a celebrated drag queen who encouraged others in the gay community to live openly, Sarria fought back.

He co-founded several new gay political and civic organizations, and by 1962 he had organized the remaining San Francisco bars into the Tavern Guild, the first gay business association in the United States,[102] whose candidate forums within a few years were attracting aspirants for the Board

---

[102] Carter, David. *Stonewall*. New York: St. Martin's Griffin. 2004 (p. 105).

of Supervisors including Willie Brown, Diane
Feinstein, and John Burton.[103] At the same time, he
helped create The League for Civil Education
(LCE), The Society for Individual Rights (SIR),
which, along with the Tavern Guild, helped undo
many of the city's anti-homosexual laws.[104] His
most enduring legacy, however, may be his
creation and supervision of the International
Court System, today a network of over seventy
separate non-profit LGBT charitable organizations in the U.S., Canada, and Mexico.
Originating with Tavern Guild's balls, the ICS
raises millions of dollars each year for charitable
causes through costume balls and drag shows. It
has a membership as large as the Human Rights
Campaign and is second only in size among LGBT
organizations to the Metropolitan Community
Church.[105]

---

[103] Ibid.

[104] Ibid. and Duberman, Martin. *Stonewall*. New York:
Penguin Books. 1994, p. 99, Demillo.

[105] Hirshman, Linda. *Victory: The Triumphant Gay
Revolution*. New York: Harper Collins. 2012, p. 279; and

Sarria built a power base by organizing through the institutions available to the gay community, and when those were threatened, he created new ones. The LGBT community has made tremendous strides in the past thirty years fighting to reclaim its place within traditional institutions including families, religious congergations, and unions, as well as creating new political advocacy groups, charitable and service organizations, university groups and student groups, and gay-owned and gay-friendly businesses.

Unfortunately, many LGBT political organizations today lack a robust institutional base, reflecting a mainstream political culture driven by large donors and individual supporters. For LGBT organizations this is the result of generations of exclusion from many civic and religious institutions. For broader progressive coalitions it's the result of a decades-long assault on unions and a generation of declining membership in mainline

---

International Court System website: http://www.impcourt.org.

religious institutions. The erosion of trust and participation in institutions, coupled with a long-atomized culture, has left most political and advocacy organizations only with a toolkit of online donations, fundraising galas, and social media activism. Taking a page from José Sarria's book, any long-term effort to organize effectively around LGBT issues should be built on the community's current institutional base with its potential for talent, grassroots network of relationships, potential to raise funding, and its moral authority.

Lesson #2: Build a Practice of Local Action
— Craig Rodwell

Amartya Sen, in his article "Democracy as a Universal Value" says that democratic partici-pation has "an *intrinsic value* for human life and well-being".[106] Like Aristotle, Sen believes we fully develop our capacity as humans through

---

[106] Sen, Amartya, *Journal of Democracy*, 10.3, 1999, pp. 3-17.

political action, where we can develop virtues like courage and judgment. This happens most effectively in the context of institutions or political organizations that focus on leadership develop- ment and are grounded in a practice of action and reflection. The homophile movement of the 1950s and 1960s was the early period of gay rights organizing in which some of the first organizations, including the Mattachine Society, Daughters of Bilitis, and ONE, Inc., fought to gain tolerance for the LGBT community and assimilation into broader society. These organizations provided the space for early activists to develop leadership skills through smaller, incremental actions that could be applied to much larger, sometimes historic ones.

An example of this is the work of Craig Rodwell, an early gay rights activist who, over the course of nearly a decade of courageous activism, prepared himself to play a crucial role in the historic riots at Stonewall in 1969. Rodwell dedicated himself to a lifetime of activism after a failed suicide attempt in his early twenties when his boyfriend, a conservative, closeted Wall Street businessman named Harvey Milk broke up with him in 1961 for fear of being outed. Rodwell was a particularly brash member of the early gay rights organization, the Mattachine Society, where he helped organize a series of annual silent demonstrations outside the White House protesting the ban against federal employment of homosexuals. The actions gained major media attention and eventually evolved into what is now the Gay Pride Parade in New York commemorating the events at Stonewall.[107] In 1966, Rodwell, along with other Mattachine members, led a series of "sip-ins" in New York modeled after the sit-ins of the Black civil rights movement. To gain media attention on New York State regulations prohibiting serving homo-sexuals in bars, Rodwell and other activists, with reporters in tow, would demand to be served as homosexuals at local pubs. After a series of sympathetic editorials and the support of the

---

[107] Duberman, pp. 113-14.

Black chairman of the New York Commission on Human Rights, the legislation was repealed.[108]

Then, on the night of June 29th, 1969, Rodwell and his boyfriend at the time were walking home and noticed a growing group of angry protestors outside the Stonewall Inn, a mafia-owned gay bar known for its mistreatment of its own patrons and frequent police raids. For the first time, bar patrons had fought back against a police crackdown, and managed to trap the officers inside the bar and pelt it with coins, rocks, and eventually a parking meter. Rodwell later said of that moment, "I knew this was the spark we had been awaiting for years."[109] Rodwell ran to a telephone booth and called his contacts from *the New York Times*, *Daily News*, and *the Post* he had carefully cultivated during the sip-ins and the White House protests. As the crowd grew over-night, he and others helped focus the protests by blocking off certain streets and intervening when

[108] Duberman, pp. 114-116.

[109] Eisenbach, David. *Gay Power: An American Revolution.* New York: Carroll and Graff. 2006. p. 95.

police began beating some of the rioters. Overnight he printed and distributed fliers with pleas to continue the protests over the coming days. The rioters' numbers swelled to a few thousand over the next few days and made national attention, marking what many consider the beginning of the modern-day gay rights movement. While there were many heroes at Stonewall, especially transgender and gender non-conforming persons of color who led the rebellion, historian David Eisenbach points to Rodwell's particular role in alerting the mainstream media in making Stonewall a historic moment: "While the riot had a huge impact on the several hundred who harassed the cops that night, more significant was the media trigger that was pulled...to the millions of homosexuals and straights, who read, saw, and heard news reports of the riot."[110]

Rodwell's preparation for Stonewall happened during the smaller actions in the preceding years, where he developed the courage, experience, and

---

[110] Ibid.

relationships needed to act when the opportunity arose. Leadership, like courage and imagination, is a skill that cannot be taught well through direct instruction but rather is cultivated through action and experience that is reflected upon. Ernesto Cortes, Jr., former National Co-Director of the Industrial Areas Foundation, likens this type of knowledge, built through action and experience within institutions, to the Greek notion of *metis*, or local knowledge, "*Metis* is not only a set of practical skills and intelligence grounded in experience, but it is used specifically in reference to the capacity to adapt to a constantly changing natural and human environment...People or institutions using metis do not assume they have correctly identified either the problem or the solution; they instead assume that only through incremental learning and constant feedback and evaluation will they understand the real issues and be able to reach long-term solutions."[111]

---

[111] Cortes, Ernesto, "Towards a Democratic Culture," *Kettering Review*, Spring 2006.

How does this framework for leadership development explain someone like Harvey Milk? He, unlike Rodwell, was not involved in gay rights organizing the first three decades of his life, yet in his forties had a meteoric rise in politics. Part of the explanation is that Milk spent much of the 1950s and 1960s developing his skills as a leader in two of the most powerful institutions in the country: the U.S. Military and Wall Street. Milk spent four years as a U.S. Naval officer after graduation from college in 1951, attending officers' training school and receiving a series of promotions including that of communications officer, lieutenant junior grade, and eventually chief petty officer of the U.S.S Kitiwake stationed in San Diego. Then, starting in the late 1950s, Milk worked for over a decade in the New York financial world, primarily at the Wall Street Firm Bache and Company where again he was promoted quickly to supervisor providing daily investment advice to branches throughout the country. Milk had successful mentors like Bach vice-president Jim Bruton, another closeted gay man who helped Milk navigate a successful career in the business world at a time when gay Wall

Street workers were the frequent targets of blackmail and extortion.[112]

Harvey Milk developed an understanding of power, money, and organization through his years of experience in the leadership-oriented military and success-driven Wall Street. Once he came to terms with his sexuality, he adapted those skills to San Francisco city politics. No doubt Milk was gifted with extraordinary charisma and smarts, but as a closeted white male, he also had the privilege and opportunities to develop leadership skills that were not open to many women, people of color, and openly LGBT persons at the time. But this proves my point: it's not just talent that's important, but also the access to institutions that form leaders and help us learn how to build and exercise power. LGBT political organizations should be the most inclusive across race, class, gender, gender identity, age, and geography, and focused on identifying, training, developing a broad and diverse base of leaders through a practice of action and reflection. There

---

[112] Shilts, pp. 23-24.

are other potential Harvey Milks out there, and a
political organization interested in developing
talent ought to have a strategy to find them.

Lesson #3: Develop a Broad Range of Issues and Allies
— Harvey Milk

In his book *Democracy and Tradition*, Princeton
University professor Jeffrey Stout talks about the
dual purpose of "broad-based organizing": "first,
to mitigate the tendency of groups organized
around singular identities to use their power to
advance only their own narrowly conceived
interests; and second, to build up coalitions with
enough power to address issues that cannot be
resolved merely by applying leverage to local
institutions.[113] Part of the solution is to resist the
temptation to focus on what LGBT organizer
Urvashi Vaid calls "an isolationist for LGBTQ
politics" focused on equal protection of individual

---

[113] Stout, Jeffrey. *Blessed Are the Organized: Grassroots
Democracy in America*. Princeton: Princeton University
Press, 2010.

rights.[114] This requires the willingness to address a broad range of issues and allies, especially among other marginalized groups. This type of coalition building was effectively used by African American civil rights groups in the 1960s, as advocated for by openly gay civil rights organizer and strategist Bayard Rustin in his essay "From Protest to Politics".

I believe Harvey Milk's distinctive contribution to LGBT history is his breadth of vision in this regard. Milk did not want to be known simply as a gay rights advocate. From the beginning of his political career, he worked to build a coalition of all disenfranchised groups, including the gay community, Hispanics, Blacks, the elderly, and unions. His broad vision is evident in his speeches: "Without hope, not only gays, but the blacks, the seniors, the handicapped, the us'es, the us'es will give up".[115] "Wake up America...No more racism, no more sexism, no more ageism, no

---

[114] Vaid, p. 31.

[115] Milk, Harvey. "Hope Speech," 1978 California Democratic Gay Caucus Dinner.

more hatred."[116] Before being elected, Milk solidified his relationships with unions by organizing the city's gay bars in support of the teamsters' successful boycott of Coors Beer. He gained an endorsement from the Mexican American Political Association. His support in the gay community came not from the well-heeled leaders of the gay political establishment that spurned him from the beginning as an interloper. Milk's base in the gay community came from the thousands of working-class gays in the Castro as well as other marginalized members of the LGBT community, including drag queens: José Sarria was the first person to endorse Milk and encouraged others to do the same.[117]

Who was the target of his political action? His particular animus was reserved for the city's elites: real estate interests, downtown corporations, and the tourism industry who all sought to turn San Francisco into a playground for the rich

---

[116] Milk, Harvey. Speech at the Gay Freedom Day Parade, 1978.

[117] Shilts, p. 149.

by converting livable neighborhoods into high-end developments, hotels, tourist attractions, and entertainment centers. Note that here Milk targeted institutional, not individual actors, reflecting a knowledge that his coalitions would only be effective if they understood the sources and nature of institutional power in the city. Milk wanted to reform the city's tax structure to make downtown livable for the elderly and low-income families. During his brief tenure as Supervisor before his assassination, Milk pushed for higher business taxes, a commuter tax for the over 300,000 corporate employees who lived outside the city, and an anti-real estate speculation tax.[118] Milk felt those who controlled wealth also had an obligation to share that prosperity with the city: "American business must realize that while the shareholders always come first, the care and feeding of their customer is a close second…. They have a debt and responsibility to the customer and the city in which he or she lives."[119]

---

[118] Shilts, pp. 193-94.

[119] Milk, Harvey. Speech at fundraising dinner, 1977.

I think there are several lessons for LGBT organizing that can be drawn from Milk's vision and how he acted on it. First, he understood the potential political power of building a real coalition of marginalized groups; he was politically shrewd and knew that if the gay community itself was organized, it could then leverage that power to build allies with other groups that shared the same experience as outsiders. Secondly, I think he understood that there is no clear separation between issues regarding sexuality, race, and economic standing. His speeches, quoted above, speak to this. Finally, Milk's identity as an outsider was formed as a closeted gay man, living in New York at one of the most oppressive times for homosexuals in Western history. Milk appeared to believe that the soul of the gay community would be shaped by how it treated other disenfranchised groups once it had access to power, as he did upon winning the election to the Board of Supervisors.

Looking Forward

There have been historic advances in the fight for equal rights for LGBT persons over the past decade including marriage equality, the repeal of the military's "Don't Ask Don't Tell" policy, and the passage of federal hate crimes legislation. While to be sure, more victories for equal rights for LGBT people are on the horizon, history can be as much cyclical as it is progressive. In her book, *The Straight State*, historian Margot Canaday documents how the middle of the twentieth century was perhaps the most repressive time for homosexuals in American History. During this time federal bans on employment, service in the military, and immigration and naturalization were implemented.[120]

It is important for any LGBT political leader to see beyond the immediate time period, and prepare for a continued, long-term organizing effort. This goal should not be just for equal rights,

---

[120] Canaday, Margo. *The Straight State*. Princeton: Princeton University Press. 2009. pp. 1-2.

but for a more just society economically, racially, and socially. The heroic efforts of LGBT activists and leaders in the latter part of the last century provide invaluable lessons in organizing for LGBT rights over the next generation: Organize institutionally, develop leadership through action, and think broadly in terms of issues and allies.

Chapter 6

The World Only Spins Forward

Stop the Bleeding

The trial of Jose Aviles[121] for the murder of Norma and Maria Hurtado began in December of 2012 and hinged on questions of intent. Aviles and his lawyer made no bones about the fact that he fired all the rounds of his automatic pistol, and that all those rounds killed Norma and Maria Hurtado. He did argue, however, that his intent was to kill Norma, and not her mother. This is relevant for Aviles because intending to kill more than one person in Texas can raise a penalty from murder, which carries the possibility of parole, to capital murder, which generally eliminates the possibility

---

[121] Beach, Patrick. "Intent In Dispute In Double-Murder Trial," *Austin American-Statesman*, December 11th, 2021.

of parole. The state was not seeking the death penalty in the Hurtado case.

Aviles' defense against capital murder was that Maria "got in the way" when he was riddling Norma with bullets. She was collateral damage, he claimed, and not part of what he planned when he approached the house. But Aviles and his lawyer confused "premeditation" with "intent". Though he may not have planned beforehand the murder of Maria Hurtado, he could certainly have intended to kill her when she got in the way.

Aviles gave his testimony in Spanish, and the Spanish phrase he used was actually a clearer connotation of Maria's own intention. Aviles said Maria "passed in front of" Norma during the shooting. Getting in the way could imply an inadvertent position of her body, or maybe she tripped in front of Norma. But "passed in front of" implies that Maria was trying to save her daughter. There are many ways a parent of an LGBT child can stand with, and protect, their child. But there will be no better example of this than what Maria did that day on Dixie Drive.

The jury didn't buy Aviles' explanation, and after just one hour of deliberation, they convicted him of capital murder, and he was sentenced to life in prison without parole.

2010 and 2011 were particularly brutal years for LGBT people in the United States. The rash of LGBT deaths by suicide and anti-gay murders was a low point in our history and one that hopefully will not be forgotten. But this same period sparked a reaction from our country that eventually led, within just a few years, to some of the most monumental LGBT civil rights victories in our country's history. I will go to my grave believing these victories were, in large part, our country's response to the countless tragedies during these two years.

It started with the "It Gets Better" movement, which was a critical intervention to give hope to staunch the immediate loss of just one more life during this time. Thousands of LGBT people and allies gave online testimonials of hope that if a teenager or young adult in despair could just hold out, chances are their lives would improve.

The entertainment industry also took a lead role, with celebrities coming out and an increasing number of LGBT characters appearing on television and in movies. Pop singers penned anthems to inclusion and diversity, like Pink's "Raise Your Glass", Katy Perry's "Firework", and Kesha's "We R Who We R".

LGBT civil rights and advocacy organizations dug in deeper in their fight at the ballot box, in state houses, city halls, and the halls of Congress. Targeted education campaigns to change public opinion were coupled with both state and federal judicial strategies to chip away at the prohibition on same-sex marriage, which became this period's defining fight. Eventually, bit by bit, state by state, public opinion changed, and statewide bans put in place over the previous decade were being overturned at breakneck speed. In 2013, the U.S. Supreme Court over-turned the Defense of Marriage Act, and finally in 2015, the Obergefell ruling legalized same-sex marriage nationwide. This was just one issue, albeit a foundational one, in the fight for LGBT civil rights. A monumental battle had been won. The next phase of the LGBT movement would be defined by the move to a broader set of issues at the intersection of socio-economic status, race, and gender, as well as transgender rights.

I was never fully satisfied with my own response to the Hurtado murders. I tried to have some conversations in my organization around this tragedy, but it was as if I couldn't quite connect the dots, partly because I had some pretty rigid categories built in my mind around issues of race, class, and sexuality at the time. I left Austin for a spell for various reasons, one of which was to pursue work in the LGBT movement. I eventually landed a position with California's statewide LGBT civil rights organization, Equality California, in 2015. My focus was to address healthcare access for LGBT undocumented immigrants in California's Central Valley. With two Latinx organizers about Norma's age named Justin and Roman, whom I supervised, we drove to cities like Bakersfield and Fresno every week to work with health clinics, immigration groups, and small LGBT Centers. I learned just as much about intersectionality from Justin and Roman as I did from the material we presented.

Norma and Maria Hurtado were among the many lives lost to anti-LGBT murder and suicide in the years surrounding April 19th, 2011. The nation witnessed, and read about, a wave of bloodshed, hate, and violence during this time. Unfortunately, it hasn't stopped. According to the Human Rights Campaign, 2021 saw at least 57 transgender and gender non-conforming people alone fatally shot or killed by other means.[122] But if the nation's response to the previous tragedies was a flourishing of advocacy, changing public opinion and acceptance, and monumental victories in LGBT civil rights, it can happen again.

---

[122] Human Rights Campaign website, "Fatal Violence against the Transgender and Gender Non-Conforming Community in 2021."

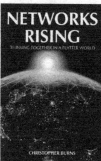

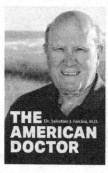
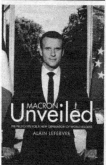